Plants
of the Tropics

written by
Susan Reading

Facts On File
New York • Oxford • Sydney

Published in the United States in 1990
by Facts On File, Inc., 460 Park Avenue South,
New York, NY 10016

A Templar book
Devised and produced by The Templar Company plc,
Pippbrook Mill, London Road, Dorking,
Surrey RH4 1JE, Great Britain

For information contact: Facts On File, Inc.,
460 Park Avenue South, New York, NY 10016

Library of Congress Cataloging-in-Publication Data

Reading, Susan.
     Plants of the tropics / Susan Reading.
        p.   cm. -- (Plant life)
     Includes bibliographical references.
     Summary: Surveys the varieties of plants that grow in
  the tropical forests of the world and describes how
  they adapt to the conditions of their environment
     ISBN 0-8160-2423-5
     1. Rain forest plants--Juvenile literature.   2. Tropical
  plants--Juvenile literature.   [1. Rain forest plants.   2.
  Tropical plants.   3. Rain forest ecology.   4.
  Ecology.]   I. Title.   II.   Series.
  QK938.F6R38   1990
  581.909'3--dc20   90-32397
                                                    CIP
                                                    AC

Facts On File books are available at special discounts
when purchased in bulk quantities for businesses,
associations, institutions or sales promotions. Please call
our Special Sales Department in New York at
212/683–2244 (dial 800/322–8755 except in NY, AK or HI).

Notes to Readers
There are some words in this book that are printed in
bold type. An explanation of them is given in the
glossary on page 58.

Editor Wendy Madgwick
Designer Mike Jolley
Illustrator Ray Hutchins and Nina O'Connell

Color separations by Positive Colour Ltd, Maldon, Essex
Printed and bound by L.E.G.O., Vicenza, Italy

10 9 8 7 6 5 4 3 2 1

Contents

Tropical Places

Some of the world's most strange and beautiful plants are found in the tropics. They are often specialized, and have become adapted to live in a tropical climate. But first, let us look at what is meant by the word tropical.

If you look on a map, you will see a line, called the equator, drawn around the center of the Earth. You will also see two other lines – one called the Tropic of Cancer that circles the earth about 1600 miles (2575 km) north of the equator and the other called the Tropic of Capricorn about 1600 miles (2575 km) south of the equator. All of the area between these two Tropics is what we mean when we talk about the tropical regions. It is here that there are some of the hottest and wettest places on Earth.

Within the tropics there are no cool seasons. The sun always rises high in the sky and each day is much the same as the next, all year round. The sun rises through a misty haze at about six o'clock in the morning. As it climbs high in the sky the mist gradually clears. At midday the sun is directly overhead and the heat is intense. Water **evaporates** from rivers and trees and rain clouds form. Every afternoon heavy rain falls and there is often thunder and lightning. Night-time, although cooler, brings no relief from the humidity.

◄*From the air a tropical rain forest looks like a continuous carpet of green leaves, broken only by the courses of the many rivers that run through it. Here the great Amazon River flows through the Amazon forest of Brazil.*

►*Beneath the canopy there are few plants growing in the dim light and the trunks of the canopy trees rise straight up.*

The layers of the forest

Tropical forests are very hot and steamy places. High overhead the tops of the trees spread out as a dense canopy of leaves through which little light can filter. Under the main canopy, smaller trees and shrubs grow to make a second, lower canopy of leaves.

Beneath the trees the air is hot and humid and very still. It is very dark and very few green plants can grow on the ground. Always there is the noise of birds and animals, the buzz of insects and the constant dripping of water. Everywhere there is water; it drips from the trees, it settles on faces and bodies, it rises as steam and can always be heard trickling and gushing in many streams and rivers. The tropical forests are the oldest undisturbed places on earth – where trees have stood for tens of millions of years!

THE SUN IN THE TROPICS

*T*here is a particular reason for the position of the Tropics of Cancer and Capricorn. The Earth spins on its axis and also around the sun. If the Earth's axis were vertical to the sun, the sun would always be directly over the equator and the climate to the north and to the south would stay the same all of the time. In fact, the Earth's axis is slightly tilted and the overhead sun is sometimes to the north and sometimes to the south of the equator. The varying position of the sun in the sky gives us our seasons.

1. Tropic of Cancer   2. equator
3. Tropic of Capricorn

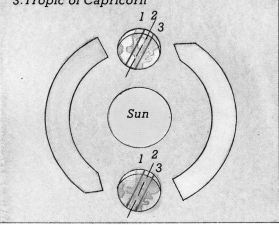

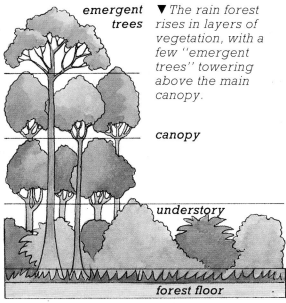

emergent trees

▼ *The rain forest rises in layers of vegetation, with a few "emergent trees" towering above the main canopy.*

canopy

understory

forest floor

Areas of Tropical Forests

Within the tropics there are three main forest areas – in Central and South America, in Asia and in Africa. The largest tropical rain forest in the world is the great Amazon forest.

It spreads across Brazil and covers the huge lowland area of the Amazon basin. The River Amazon carries the largest volume of water of any river in the world, not only because of the high rainfall but also because of the vast amount of water that flows from the melting ice, high in the Andes mountains of Peru.

The wettest rain forest in the world is called the Chocó and it is on the north-west coast of South America. There is also a long strip of rain forest that runs along the east coast of Brazil. Sadly, a lot of this has been cleared and little undisturbed forest remains.

The countries of Central America, between Mexico and Colombia, form a "bridge" between North and South America. The forests here are most dense

◄*Many small rivers run through the highland rain forests of Malaysia.*

▼ *The River Congo lies at the heart of the forest regions of Africa.*

THE DIFFERENT SORTS OF FORESTS

There are three main types of tropical forest:

1. The hottest and wettest places in the world are in the lowland regions around the equator. Here, every day is the same, without any cool seasons. The forests that grow here are called the tropical rain forests and they contain the densest vegetation in the world.

2. As you move away from the equator, the intense heat and wetness gradually gives way to cooler climates, where temperatures are slightly lower

and the rainfall more seasonal. Here, dry seasons alternate with heavy monsoon rains. The rain forests in these areas are called seasonal or monsoon forests.

3. Rising above the intensely hot lowlands there are mountain ranges. Even near the equator, conditions in the mountains are much cooler and less humid than lower down. The rising water vapor condenses out in the cooler air as mist and fog, and the forests here are called cloud forests.

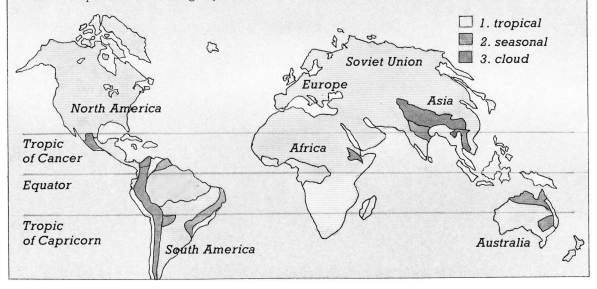

1. tropical
2. seasonal
3. cloud

on the Pacific side because of the higher rainfall. Farther east are the heavily forested tropical islands of the Caribbean, such as Jamaica and Puerto Rico.

Forests of Asia and Africa

Asia has a lot of tropical rain forests, particularly in Southeast Asia and the many islands of Malaysia and Indonesia. At one time most of Indo-China was covered by rain forest, but over the years much of this forest has been cut down and the land used for cultivating crops. Forest areas are now patchy.

The forests of Africa spread across that hugh continent from the great "bite" called the Gulf of Guinea into the countries

of West and Central Africa. At the heart of these forests is the River Congo – the second longest river in Africa. The forests end where mountain ranges rise up in the north and east.

Other forest areas

The northern part of Australia lies within the tropics. Rain forests occur in Queensland, although they are not so rich in plant and animal life as the forests in other parts of the world.

North America has its tropical forests too, in the swamps of the Everglades, at the tip of Florida. They are of great scientific interest and are preserved as a National Park.

9

The Richness of Life

Tropical forests have the densest plant growth found anywhere in the world, and have some of the tallest trees and the greatest variety of plants.

Conditions for growth are obviously favorable but, for some plants, forest life presents many difficulties that have to be overcome. Before we look at the special problems of tropical forest plants, let us take a brief look at the things that all plants need if they are to grow.

What plants need for food

The basic needs of a plant are simple – air, water, warmth, light and a supply of minerals. Most plants have to make their own food to survive. They do this by a process known as **photosynthesis**, which generally takes places in the leaves.

Water from the ground taken up by the plant's roots and carbon dioxide gas from the air are combined within the plant's cells to form sugars and oxygen. The plant uses the sugars for food but has no use for most of the oxygen, which is released back into the atmosphere. This process requires energy and plants get this from sunlight, which is trapped and stored by a green pigment called **chlorophyll**.

So, from just air, water, minerals and sunlight, plants are able to manufacture all the food that they require. The sugars combine with minerals to form carbohydrates, fats and starches, which many plants store in their roots, stems or leaves.

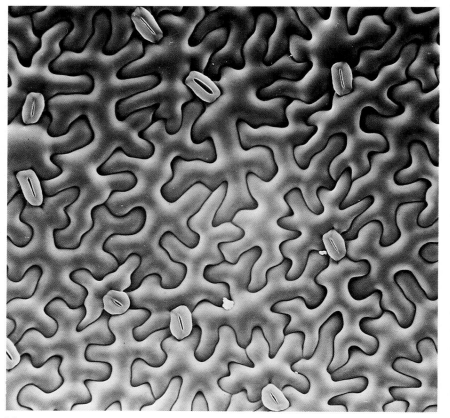

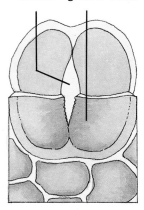

◄ *Plants' leaves have many tiny pores in their surface, through which gases and moisture pass. Each opening, or stoma, is surrounded by guard cells which open or close it as required.*

stoma   guard cells

Leaves and the air that we breathe

The surface of a leaf has many tiny pores called **stomata**. Carbon dioxide gas, which is needed in photosynthesis, enters the leaf through the stomata and oxygen is released back into the atmosphere in the same way. This happens during the day, when there is sunlight to provide energy. Without plants, no animals could survive on this planet for they depend on plants for the oxygen in the air that they breathe.

In order to use their food, all living things require oxygen. This is true of plants as well as animals. Like animals, plants also "breathe," taking in oxygen through the stomata and releasing carbon dioxide. However, the amount of oxygen that plants use during this process, called respiration, is very little compared to the much larger amount that they produce during photosynthesis.

While the stomata are open, water vapor evaporates through the openings into the air. To prevent the plant from wilting, water has to be taken up through the roots to replace that lost through the stomata, so there is a constant upward flow of water through the plant. This process is called **transpiration**.

▼ *A constant upward flow of water replaces that which is lost through evaporation during transpiration.*

evaporation

water

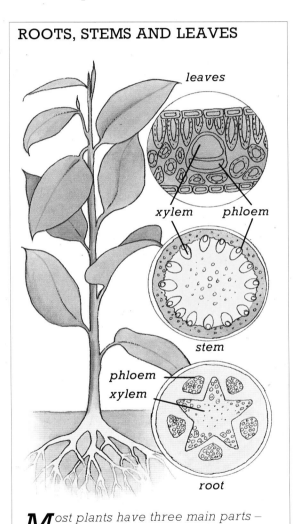

ROOTS, STEMS AND LEAVES

leaves

xylem   phloem

stem

phloem
xylem

root

*M*ost plants have three main parts – roots, stems and leaves.
*The roots anchor the plant to the ground and keep it steady. They absorb water and minerals from the soil. The water and minerals are transported up the stem from the roots, through a network of veins called the vascular system, to the leaves. Water is carried in the **xylem** cells. The food made in the leaves is taken around the plant in **phloem** cells.*

Life on the Forest Floor

On the forest floor the atmosphere is hot, humid and stagnant, for there is little circulation of air. There are very few green plants here, because the light is blotted out by the canopy above and is too dim for photosynthesis.

Most of the plants of the forest floor are either **saprophytes** that obtain their food from dead and rotting plants, or **parasites** that grow on other living plants and take food from them.

Saprophytes

Most of the forest saprophytes are fungi. They are very important because they break down decaying plant material and recycle the nutrients back into the soil.

The main part of a fungus is the feeding body or **mycelium**, which consists of a network of thread-like strands called **hyphae**. The mycelium spreads underground and throughout the dead plant material. Fungi reproduce by spores, which are made in the "fruiting bodies."

Fruiting bodies come in many different forms, but mushrooms and toadstools are probably the ones that we know best.

Some tropical fungi are very beautiful. Maiden's veil, for instance, has an intricate lace-like veil that only lasts for one day. Insects are attracted to its sticky cup by its ghastly smell! Many tropical fungi, such as *Mycena cyanophos*, glow in the dark. Fairy club fungi produce tiny tree-like structures in a dazzling array of yellows, reds and scarlets. *Mycena viscid cruenta* produces masses of miniature, bright red toadstools. Species of *Tremella* in Australia have jelly-like fruiting bodies.

Not all saprophytic plants are fungi. *Thismia*, one of the very few flowering saprophytes, produces masses of star-like flowers.

Parasites

Parasites on the forest floor get their food second-hand from other plants, which are known as hosts. Some of the most wide-spread parasitic plants are the dodders. Dodders are found almost everywhere throughout the world and tropical rain forests are no exception. They penetrate into their hosts with root-like structures called **haustoria**. These link up with the xylem and phloem cells in the host's stem and take water and nourishment from them. Another plant parasite, *Thonningia sanguinea*, produces bright red flowers and is a common sight on forest floors.

▼ *Fungi come in all shapes and sizes from microscopic molds to large mushrooms and toadstools.*

◄ *Dodders are strange looking plants. They have a tangle of reddish stems that spread and twine over their hosts and masses of pink flowers.*

A WORLD RECORD FLOWER

*T*he largest flower in the world is produced by a parasite called Rafflesia. *Species of* Rafflesia *are widespread throughout the tropics, but it is the Asian variety that is the record holder. For most of its life* Rafflesia *is not visible outside its host plant. It has no real leaves or stem and consists of masses of filaments that grow inside the roots of its host – a forest vine.*

The flowers have thick, leathery petals, speckled red, brown and white, and have a strong smell of rotting meat that attracts flies. Their seeds are dispersed on the feet of large animals which tread on the vines and damage them. The Rafflesia *seeds get pressed into the squashed vines and start to grow.*

The only part of the Rafflesia *plant that you normally see is the enormous, evil-smelling flowers. These flowers can grow to be about 3 feet (1 meter) across and weigh 20 pounds (9 kg).*

Plants of the Forest Floor

Life on the tropical forest floor is far from easy and few green plants grow there. There are no **annuals** or **bulbs** because there are no seasons. Growth continues all the year and plants have no need to survive bad times as dormant bulbs or seeds.

Lack of light is the main problem for green plants. The canopy of leaves makes an almost solid barrier to the sun and less than 5 percent of the sunlight reaches the ground. When it does get through, it is a dim, green light or occasional dappled patches.

There is very little circulation of air, and it is hot and humid all of the time, both day and night, with hardly any variation in the temperature.

In this vast plant world, the amount of carbon dioxide in the air is low. This is because so much is being used in photosynthesis by the millions of leaves above. The plants that grow here often have their stomata raised above the leaf surface to make it easier for them to absorb the carbon dioxide that they need.

Tropical grasses

Grasses that grow on the forest floor do not look like the long-leaved, narrow grasses of temperate regions. In order to get as much light as they can, these grasses have long, broad leaves and look very much like the other plants of the forest. They are very efficient at photosynthesis and are able to survive better than most other plants where there is not much carbon dioxide.

Ferns

Ferns are particularly good at surviving in dim and dark places because their divided fronds can catch the maximum amount of light. Many delicate ferns, such

◀Dark green leaves, large broad leaves and leaves that are angled to catch the light are all helpful to plants that grow in dark places.

▶Some plants grow as small herbs in temperate woodland, but are so well suited to life in tropical forests that they can reach tree-like proportions. The South American tree violet, Rinorea, and giant tree ferns (shown here) can grow to 30 feet (10 meters).

▼ *The delicate,*
divided fronds of
ferns make the best
use of the dim light.

as maidenhair ferns, or the bird's nest fern
with its long, elegant leaves, can be found
on the forest floor. Some ferns can grow to
be large plants, like the giant tree ferns
which can reach a height of about 30 feet
(10 meters).

LEAVES OF THE DARK

*I*n a dark world it is hard for a plant to
make enough food, because light is
essential for photosynthesis. It helps if
their leaves have a large amount of the
green pigment chlorophyll to trap the
light. The leaves of tropical forest
plants are often large, broad and very
dark green with extra pigment to make
the best use of the dim light. This is
clearly seen in many climbing plants,
including members of the large arrow-
root family.

Leaves of ground cover plants like
the Hawaiian Broussaisia arguta are
arranged in rosettes. Each leaf is set at
the best angle to receive the maximum
amount of light, and arranged so as not
to shade any of the other leaves.

The Lower Canopy

Conditions in the lower canopy are similar to the conditions found on the florest floor. The main canopy cuts out most of the sunlight and the light is dim and green. Here there is less variation in temperature than in the main canopy, and less rain. The air is hot, humid and still.

Some of the plants here are young trees whose growth has been halted by a lack of light. Others are small, fully-grown trees, shrubs and palms which may be as much as 163 feet (50 meters) tall.

Trees and shrubs of the lower canopy generally have elongated crowns. Each leaf is set at the best angle to receive as much light as possible. Most of the leaves have a special swollen joint at the base of each stalk, called a **pulvinus**. The stalks are sensitive to light and rotate the leaves to follow the sun as it moves daily from east to west.

Brightly colored leaves

The young leaves of the lower and the upper canopy trees have one unusual feature that is only found in tropical plants. When they are first formed, they come in a range of brilliant colors, from red, purple to blue and even white. The leaves do not turn green until they are older. It is

▲ *Typical trees of the lower canopy have elongated crowns. The young leaves often hang down limply.*

The young leaves with their many colors give brilliance to the dark, monotonous blanket of green.

thought that these colored pigments shield the more delicate green chlorophyll until the leaf is fully mature.

Some useful trees

Many trees and shrubs of the lower canopy are unnamed. Some, however, have proved useful to man and are more familiar. They are often cultivated.

The wild avocado tree, for instance, is common in the tropical forests of America. The clove tree, *Syzygium aromaticum*, a forest shrub of the myrtle family, is widely cultivated as a spice.

Bulnesia sarmienti is a small, stunted tree which seldom grows to more than

15 feet (5 meters) and is harvested for its aromatic oils. *Citrus aurantium*, an orange tree, also produces an exotic scented oil. The drug reserpine is extracted from *Rauwolfia*, an evergreen shrub found in African, Asian and American rain forests.

Useful palms

Most of the 3500 species of palms originated in tropical forests. It is one of the groups of plants most useful to man and many of them are now cultivated.

Elaeis guineensis, the West African oil palm, is grown for its oil which is used in cooking oil, margarine and soap. *Metroxylon sagu*, the sago palm of Southeast Asia, has starch deposits in its trunk, which are heated to make pearl sago. *Arenga saccharifera* is the Malaysian sugar palm and is the source of a thick, sugary syrup.

Raffia, which is used for baskets, comes from a Madagascan palm called *Raphia ruffia*. *Copernicia cerifera*, a Brazilian palm, produces a wax used in polishes.

ANCIENT TREES

*C*ycads are ancient conifers that look very much like palm trees. They are common beneath the main canopy and have grown in tropical forests almost unchanged for the last 200 million years!

▼ These are some of the useful palms that originated in tropical forests and are now cultivated.

oil palm

wax palm

17

The Main Canopy

The trees that make up the main canopy of the forest reach up with long, straight, unbranched trunks, 130–160 feet (40 to 50 meters) high. At the top their branches radiate outwards to make a thick, continuous layer of leaves.

◀ *The dense canopy of leaves may be as much as 18–22 feet (6 or 7 meters) deep.*

▼ *Many tropical leaves are dark green and shiny with "drip-tips" to shed water.*

In temperate woodlands, different sorts of trees have evolved to deal with different conditions – summer, winter, light and shade, dry and damp. In tropical forests the conditions are the same all of the time, and many of the trees and their leaves look very similar.

Canopy leaves

With so many trees crowded together, all trying to get enough carbon dioxide, light and minerals to live, it is vital for the leaves to be in tip-top condition.

Canopy leaves are all dark green with extra chlorophyll. They are shiny and hard, with a thick waxy coating so that the water drops can run off easily from their surface. Many have special "drip-tips" so that the rainwater can drain away. Damp, soggy leaves would soon become covered in mosses, molds or algae. If the stomata clogged, the trees could not get enough carbon dioxide from the air. Also, if the water did not evaporate from the leaves, there would be less water rising up the plant to carry minerals from the roots to the leaves.

Dealing with epiphytes

All canopy trees have many **epiphytes** growing on them. Some trees try to stop their growth by having poisonous bark

TREES WITH NO NAMES

Canopy trees are so tall that we often do not know what sort of trees they are. Many of them have never been identified or named. Botanists have been known to try to shoot branches down with arrows, or even to train monkeys to climb up and fetch branches down for examination! Modern tree-climbing methods make the task a little easier. Even so, a lot of canopy trees can only be identified by cutting the bark and looking at the sap, or recognizing the smell or color.

which prevents the seedlings germinating. Others, like *Terminalia* and *Bursera*, have bark that flakes off from time to time, which causes the epiphytes to fall off too. Sometimes trees benefit from epiphytes by growing special roots from their branches. These penetrate the epiphytes and take minerals from them.

Roots for food and support

Canopy trees are very large and heavy. Apart from their own weight, they also support the extra burden of epiphytic and parasitic plants.

Because the soil is shallow, with most of the nutrients close to the surface, the feeding roots do not go very deep into the soil. Extra roots are needed to anchor the trees and prevent them from falling. There are special supporting roots that are found in tropical forest trees, and nowhere else.

Some, called buttress roots, grow from as high as 30 feet (10 meters) up the trunk, spreading like giant wings outwards to the forest floor. Other trees have a mass of roots, called stiltroots, that hang down from the trunk, looking like the guy ropes of a tent.

▼ *Buttress roots and stiltroots are only found in tropical forests.*

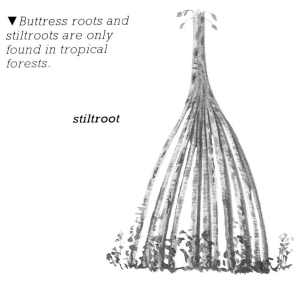

stiltroot

buttress root

The Emergent Layer

Some trees grow even taller than those of the main canopy and tower high above the rest of the forest. These are called emergent trees.

Up above the canopy living conditions are very different from those found lower down. Here, the humid heat and airlessness of the canopy is replaced by fresher, drier winds and the full force of the sun's burning rays.

Dry at the top

In this drier air there is always a danger of the leaves drying out. To stop too much water loss, emergent trees have much smaller and waxier leaves than canopy trees. Some have two different kinds of leaves; small ones on the upper branches and large, broad leaves lower down, where they merge with the rest of the dense canopy.

High trees and wide trees

It is often said that tropical rain forest trees are the tallest in the world, but this is not strictly true. The tallest tropical tree is the

▶ *Seeds of emergent trees are carried on the wind. The giant kapok of South America produces masses of fluffy seeds which can drift for miles. Dipterocarpus seeds are wafted through the air on wings formed by enlarged sepals. Melanorrhea has seeds with five radiating wings which helps them drift over the canopy far away from the parent plant.*

giant kapok

Dipterocarpus

◀ *The emergent trees rise above the top of the canopy. Their branches radiate upwards in dome-shaped crowns.*

Melanorrhea

tualang, *Koompassia excelsa*, of Southeast Asia. This has been known to reach 272 feet (90 meters). Most of the canopy trees reach about 200 feet (62 meters).

The real giants among trees are not tropical at all. The Australian *Eucalyptus regnans* and the Californian redwood, *Sequoia sempervirens*, hold the world record for height and both can reach well over 360 feet (120 meters)!

The East Indian fig tree is one of the largest trees in the world, even though it is not particularly tall – only 100 feet (30 meters). It is large because it spreads to a great width and can cover acres of ground. There is a record of one specimen that was 2,000 feet (620 meters) across and, it is said, was able to give shelter to 7,000 people! Surprisingly, the fig starts life as an epiphyte, growing on other trees, and then sends roots downwards to the ground.

Drifting seeds above the canopy

Above the main canopy of the forest, the drier winds carry the seeds of the emergent trees. Many of these seeds are shaped or winged to float on the air currents. They may drift for miles before they finally sink to the ground.

THE EVENLY GROWING TRUNK

*T*rees of temperate regions do their growing in the spring and summer and stay dormant in the winter. This spurt of growth, followed by a rest period, shows in the wood of the trunk. A cross section of the trunk of a temperate tree shows annual growth rings, each one being the new growth of vascular tissue for one year. If you count these rings you can tell how old a tree is. Growth rings will be broad if it was a good year for growth, but bad years produce narrower rings.

In the tropics, trees grow all year round. The wood of the trunk grows evenly, with no spurts of growth, and no rings.

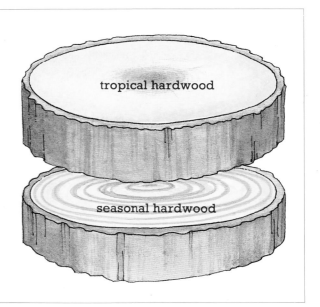

tropical hardwood

seasonal hardwood

When a Tree Falls

Although forest plants grow with such speed and vigor, the soil is not at all fertile. Few nutrients are found in the soil itself, which is shallow. They are all soaked up by the lush vegetation and are contained within the plants themselves.

In temperate woodlands, most of the trees are deciduous. When winter arrives they shed their leaves and rest until the better weather returns.

In tropical rain forests, most trees are evergreen. There is no cold season to stop their growth and they grow all the year round. The older leaves are shed and replaced with new ones throughout the year. When the leaves fall they rot very quickly, within about six weeks, because of the many bacteria and fungi in the soil. In this way the minerals and nutrients are ready to be used again almost immediately.

The fall of a tree

Sometimes a large tree crashes to the ground. Perhaps it is because of old age or disease. It may even be due to the weight of climbing plants and epiphytes

◀ The weight of epiphytic plants growing on a tree can sometimes be so great as to cause the tree to fall.

▶ Fallen trees leave a gap through which the light will stream.

growing on it. Sometimes thunderstorms, high winds or volcanic activity topples trees. Whatever the cause, the fall of a forest tree brings about sudden activity in the plants and animals of the forest floor.

When the light shines in

The fall of a tree unexpectedly brings light to the dark regions below. There, tree seedlings that have grown just a little at the start of their life wait in a state of suspended animation for just such an opportunity. Light is now flooding through the canopy and the seedlings begin to grow.

The first trees to reach the top of the canopy will be the ones to survive. Their branches will spread to fill the gap and take all the light. The less successful trees will become weaker as they are deprived of light and eventually they will die.

Activity on the forest floor

While the seedlings are racing to the top, the fallen tree will be creating further activity on the forest floor. White ants or termites arrive in hoards. Termites are able to digest the cellulose that makes up woody parts of the tree. With their help, the wood decomposes and the minerals are released back into the soil.

With so much rain, the minerals can easily be washed away. The healthy standing trees have to be quick to absorb the minerals before this happens. Each tree has a thick mat of spreading rootlets which soaks up the minerals like a sponge as soon as they become available.

▼ *Termites form well organized colonies. They burrow their way through the trunks of fallen trees.*

Interconnecting chambers – some are used as brood chambers, others for storing debris.

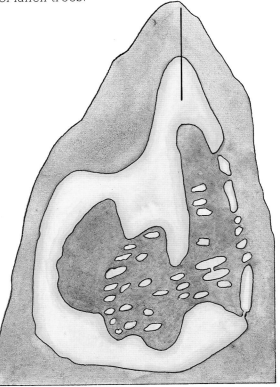

Epiphytes

Hardly a tree can be found in the tropics that does not have many other plants growing on it. These plants take nothing from the tree but support; the tree itself does not usually benefit in any way.

◄ The lichen Usnea *can withstand drier conditions than most other epiphytes. The long white drooping strands of this plant lead to it being known as old man's beard.*

▼ Canopy trees often support many epiphytes, and sometimes their thick waxy leaves are covered in unusual flat, star-shaped patterns. These are not part of the leaves, but are due to the growth of small leafy liverworts, known as **microphylls**.

Sometimes so many of these plants grow on a tree that their weight may be enough to bring a branch, or even the whole tree, crashing to the ground. They can grow low down on the trunk of the tree, or higher up on the branches and leaves. Plants that grow on other plants are known as epiphytes.

Why grow on trees?

The main advantage of growing high up is that the plants are nearer to the sunlight and can avoid grazing animals. However, there are many difficulties imposed by this form of existence. Water and minerals are hard to obtain, and many epiphytes have adapted to save water in the same way as some desert plants. For example, the leaves are often protected by a waxy

coat and some plants have small leaves or no leaves at all.

The stems or roots of the plants are sometimes modified to carry out photosynthesis or to collect and store water. They can store enough water to help them survive during a dry period. Other plants survive a drought phase in a dormant or resting state, only resuming growth when water becomes available.

The lush green haze

Trunks and branches often appear to be covered in a soft felty green cloth. This is caused by heavy growths of mosses or lichens. These growths are particularly evident in cloud forests, where fog keeps the air permanently moist or humid. They may also be seen covering rocks and fallen debris on the forest floor. Even the branches of emergent trees growing in a less humid position carry their share of epiphytes.

▼ *Branches drip with pale green draperies of club mosses, such as* Lycopodium *and* Asplenium *ferns as shown below which thrive in these humid conditions.*

COLLECTING FOOD

Species of Asplenium *are commonly known as birds nest ferns. These grow in a manner designed to trap water, and animal and plant debris. The leaves are tightly packed at the base*

birds nest fern

stag's horn fern

and fan out forming a conical shaped cup. This collects pieces of leaf litter which rot in the watery vessel. Roots from the base of the plant grow through into this cup to reach a supply of water and minerals.

The stags horn or Platycerium *produces two different types of leaves. The forked leaves, which resemble stags horns, spread outwards from the stem. They function as normal leaves and carry spores. The leaves at the base of the fern spread out to form a platform over the trunk of the tree. Leaf litter and debris that collect in these is slowly broken down into a rich nutritious humus. This can absorb and retain large quantities of water. The roots of the fern grow into this humus allowing the ferns to reach a considerable size.*

Epiphytic Orchids and Cacti

Orchids are spectacular plants and half of all known species are epiphytes. Most forest cacti grow up in the trees as epiphytes, but a few grow on the ground.

The biggest problem that epiphytes have to face is getting enough water. Orchids are often very "fleshy" plants. During times of rain they are able to take up plenty of water into their stems, roots and leaves, and store it there for use during dry periods. Their leaves are thick, sometimes almost cylindrical, and waxy. The stomata are on the underside of the leaves, where less water will evaporate.

Unusual roots

Most epiphytic orchids have green chlorophyll in their roots so that photosynthesis can take place here as well as in the leaves. The roots are protected by a layer

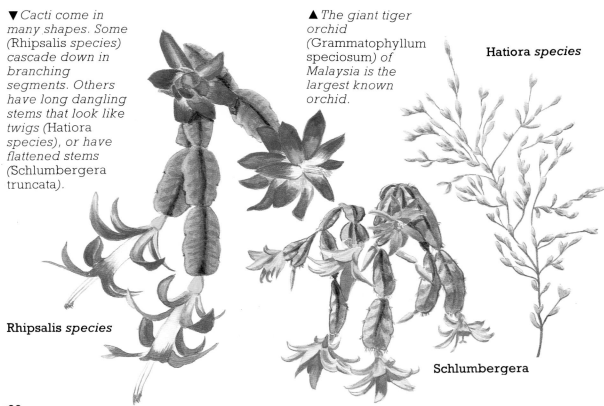

▼ *Cacti come in many shapes. Some* (Rhipsalis *species) cascade down in branching segments. Others have long dangling stems that look like twigs (*Hatiora species*), or have flattened stems (*Schlumbergera truncata).*

▲ *The giant tiger orchid* (Grammatophyllum speciosum) *of Malaysia is the largest known orchid.*

Hatiora *species*

Rhipsalis *species*

Schlumbergera

of dead cells, called the **velamen**. When the root is dry, these cells become white and reflect the light so that it cannot get through to the cells beneath. When the velamen gets wet again, the dead cells absorb water and pass it through to the storage tissue of the root beneath. The velamen also becomes transparent and allows the light through to the chlorophyll so that photosynthesis can begin.

Taeniophyllum, an orchid of Malaysia, has large, flat, green roots spreading over the bark of its host. These roots have completely taken over the task of photosynthesis and the leaves are reduced to small scales.

Pseudobulbs

Many orchids have swollen leaf bases, called pseudobulbs. These may be tiny, but sometimes they are very large – over 3 feet (1 meter) across. Water is stored here, as elsewhere in the plant. If the pseudobulb becomes detached from the rest of the plant, it is able to produce roots and grow into a whole new plant. This sort of reproduction, without seeds, is called vegetative reproduction.

Amazing flowers

Reproduction by seeds (sexual reproduction; see p. 34) is the same in orchids as in all flowering plants – except that orchid flowers are often very strange and beautiful. They have all sorts of weird and wonderful ways of attracting insects and making sure that the insects collect enough pollen to take to the next flower.

Tropical cacti

Although most forest cacti grow as epiphytes, some may be found rooted in rock crevices where leaf debris has collected. They are tough plants, well able to absorb and store water. Many have flattened stems to increase their surface to the light.

Desert cacti often have fearsome spines or prickles to reduce water loss and protect them from grazing animals. High in the forest, spines are not necessary and so they are reduced to small hairs or are absent altogether.

Most cactus seeds are spread by birds. They are usually sticky and contained in tempting, fleshy fruit. Birds eat the fruit and wipe their beaks on the tree branches. The seeds stick to the bark, where they begin to grow. Any seeds that are eaten are not harmed by the bird's digestive system and are excreted with the bird's droppings.

▼ *Some orchids, like the tropical butterfly orchid (Epidendrum tampense) of Florida, resemble insects. Male insects fly to the flowers, thinking they are mates, and get covered in pollen in the "rough and tumble."*

Bromeliads

Bromeliads are very strange plants. They are members of the pineapple family and are **monocarpic**. This means that, although bromeliads often live for a long time, they only flower once in their lifetime.

Like all epiphytes, bromeliads face the problem of getting enough water and minerals to live on. They solve this problem by making small "water tanks" out of their leaves.

Ponds of their own

The leaves of bromeliads grow in a circle, tightly pressed together and fanning out at the top. They make vase-shaped containers or urns. This is why the bromelaids are called urn, tank or vase plants.

The leaves are waxy and hard, often ending in dagger-sharp points. At their base there are little flaps called **trichomes** that open when it is wet to allow the water into special hollows in the leaf. When it is dry, the flaps contract and close down tightly to prevent water from escaping. The roots of bromeliads are used mainly for anchorage.

Life in bromeliad pools

Some of the larger bromeliad urns can hold up to about 12 gallons (55 liters) of water, enough to supply the needs of the plant as well as many animals. All sorts of plant debris collects in the urns, and decays to give valuable nutrients. This provides food for the bromeliad and also for a host of small creatures like mosquito larvae, small crabs, worms and snails that live in these ponds. Some of the larger urns are homes for even larger animals like salamanders and tree frogs.

Sometimes bromeliads have small carnivorous plants like bladderworts growing inside their urns. They catch and feed on the unsuspecting animals that live in the pool.

▲ *Tillandsia usneoides is called Spanish moss or old man's beard. Although it looks like a moss, it is a bromeliad. It hangs in huge, silver draperies from trees and rocks. In Florida, it can even be seen hanging from telegraph wires. It does not have any roots and absorbs all its water and nutrients from the air, through small scales on the stem.*

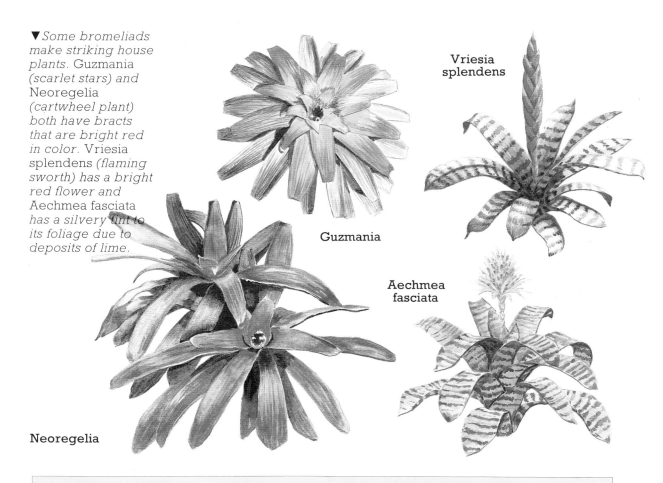

▼ *Some bromeliads make striking house plants. Guzmania (scarlet stars) and Neoregelia (cartwheel plant) both have bracts that are bright red in color. Vriesia splendens (flaming sworth) has a bright red flower and Aechmea fasciata has a silvery tint to its foliage due to deposits of lime.*

Vriesia
splendens

Guzmania

Aechmea
fasciata

Neoregelia

DEADLY FROGS

*M*any frogs and toads have poison glands in their skin, but the most poisonous of all are the arrow-poison frogs of Central and South America. So deadly is the poison that the South American Indians use it to coat their arrows, and any animals struck by the arrow soon dies.

The eggs of the frogs are carried around by the male frogs until they hatch into tadpoles. When the tadpoles get too big for his back, the frog looks for a suitable pool. He often chooses the urn of a bromeliad as a nursery. After checking that there are no other tadpoles in residence, he allows the youngsters to slide into the water. Here they live until they turn into frogs, the insect larvae and other water creatures providing all the food that they need.

The Stranglers

One of the more sinister groups of plants found in the world's rain forests are the stranglers. These plants have been described as "vegetable boa constrictors" because they kill their host trees by strangulation. Most of them are members of the *Ficus*, or fig, family.

The fruits of stranglers are relished by all sorts of animals – bats, birds, squirrels and monkeys. The seeds from these fruits are often deposited high up in the branches of the trees, in humus-filled crevices. Here, where there is plenty of light, the strangler seeds start to grow.

They start their life as epiphytes and, like all epiphytes, they find it a problem to get enough water. Strangler figs have thick waxy leaves, which helps to reduce water loss. At first, growth is very slow.

As they get bigger, they start to produce aerial roots which knit together to form a tight mesh around the trunk of the host tree. The roots lengthen and grow downwards until they eventually reach the ground below. Water and minerals can now be obtained more easily.

The killing process

Growth of the strangler fig is now very rapid, as it takes more and more water and nutrients from the soil. From this point the host tree faces ever increasing com-

◀ *The host tree is surrounded by a tightly clinging mesh of aerial roots belonging to the strangler fig.*

▲ *Eventually the strangler fig will stand alone, supporting itself in the shape of its original host.*

THE FALL OF A STRANGLED GIANT

*I*t may be that the effect of the strangler so weakens the host tree that it is ready to fall. Add to this the heavy weight of the strangler fig and the other epiphytes growing on it, and the stricken tree will come crashing to the ground.

Light then floods in from above, bringing a golden opportunity to the seeds and dormant seedlings on the ground. The fallen tree must be replaced, and the race will be won by the first plants to reach the top.

Sometimes it is the climbing cucumber, which often grows along the edges of the forests or river banks. Their fruits are often brightly colored reds and yellows. Some may even have vividly striped orange and black fruits to attract animals.

petition from the strangler. It begins to weaken through lack of nutrients and water from the soil below and a lack of sufficient light from above. Finally, the tight mesh of roots around the base of the trunk strangles the host, which dies.

One tree replaced by another

When the host tree finally dies, a process that may take 100 years, the tree trunk will slowly rot away. In the end, the strangler fig stands alone, supported by its own lattice of woody roots – like a ghost in the shape and size of its original host. One tree has been replaced by another.

▶ *Although the true stranglers are mostly of the fig family, there are others, such as the Swiss cheese plant (*Monstera deliciosa) *and climbers like* Raphidophora *that produce a mass of aerial roots that cling for support to the trunk of their host plant.*

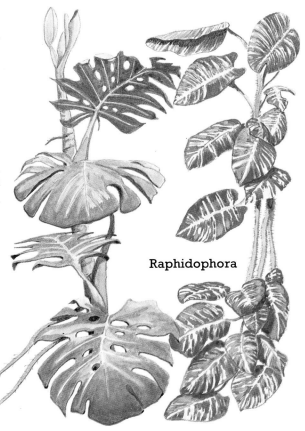

Raphidophora

Swiss cheese plant

Forest Climbers

Anyone who has seen a Tarzan film will remember him swinging from tree to tree on vines that look for all the world like hanging ropes. These are the lianas, giant climbing plants that loop through the high trees of tropical rain forests.

Lianas stretch from the forest floor to the canopy above and form a tangled mass that binds the forest trees together.

Usually we picture a tree as a high standing, woody plant, with a trunk and branches. Lianas are, in fact, trees that have lost their own strengthening tissue and rely on other trees for support. Most of their energy is used to produce the long stems that take them up into the canopy, where they weave their way through the branches and vegetation.

Lianas are the longest trees in the world. An average specimen is about 980 feet (300 meters) long, which is three times the height of the tallest rain forest tree. Some of them are much longer than that. Malaysian rattans, which are used to make light-weight furniture, may reach an extraordinary 650 feet (200 meters) in length!

Passengers to the top

Liana seeds germinate in the soil. If there is nothing near to support it, the young seedling will grow into a small bush which produces flowers and seeds like other plants. However, if it finds a support, the liana will quickly fasten on to it. Such support is often provided by sapling trees, which grow towards the canopy and take the young lianas with them.

Lianas stay rooted on the forest floor and take their water and minerals from the soil. These nutrients are carried an immense distance up to the leaves above in well developed conductive tissue.

Twisting, looping stems

The stems of these climbers do not have to be as strong as the trunks of self-supporting trees, but they do have to be tough and flexible. They grow in great loops so that they do not stretch tight and snap as the canopy branches sway in the wind. The woody, supporting tissue of the stems grows in bands, separated by layers of spongy connective tissue.

The stems are often strangely shaped. Some may be round, some may be flattened into long ribbons. They may be twisted, lobed or grooved.

Although lianas do not take any nutrients from the host trees, they produce dense growths of leaves in the canopy. The host tree is sometimes deprived of sunlight, and may weaken and die.

Philodendron

◄*Lianas have thick, strong stems. Some lianas are known as "monkey ladders." The stem edges stay straight and rigid while the middle of the stem rises in wavy undulations forming "steps."*

◄*The climbing stems have many different ways of holding on to the tree trunks. Some climbing lilies have leaf tendrils, rattans have tendrils with pointed barbs, Acacia lacerans has hooked prickles and climbing begonias have pronged projections. Philodendrons hang on with aerial roots.*

HISSING STEMS

*T*o get enough water to the top of the canopy, liana stems have a lot of water-conducting tissue. The water travels faster in liana stems than in any other plant. About two-thirds of a pint of water travels upwards every hour, at a speed of 8 feet (2.5 meters) a minute! There is such a strong force drawing this water up that if you cut a stem it hisses loudly as the air is sucked into it.

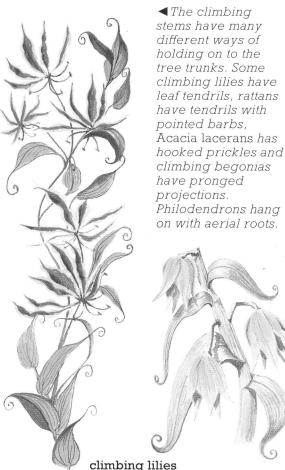

climbing lilies

Tropical Flowers

The flowers of tropical plants come in all shapes and sizes, but they all have the same job to do. They produce the male sex cell (**pollen**) and female sex cell (**ovule**).

During **pollination**, pollen is carried from the male **stamen** to the female **stigma**. The male cell grows down the **style** and fuses with or **fertilizes** the ovule in the ovary to produce a **seed**. This process is called **sexual reproduction**, and ensures that the new seedlings are different from the parent plant.

Different methods of pollination

Many plants are pollinated by the wind, but this would not be very successful in tropical forests as there is little or no wind beneath the canopy and plants of the same species are often a long way apart. Almost all pollination is carried out by insects or other animals.

Flowers attract animals by their shape, color or scent. You can often tell what sort of creature will pollinate a flower by looking at it. Many flowers have radiating patterns and colored stripes called honey guides which direct bees and other creatures towards the nectar. Some can only be seen by insect eyes as they only show up in ultraviolet light which insects can detect but which humans cannot. Plants and the animals that pollinate them have become adapted to each other.

◄ *Swallowtail butterflies are particularly attracted to red flowers.*

► *Brightly colored sunbirds take up acrobatic positions as they probe deep into flowers with their long curved beaks.*

Flowers to suit

In the dim light of the forest floor, most flowers are pale and strongly scented so that nocturnal animals can locate them. Flowers that are visited by bats have to be tough to withstand the weight of the bats and their sharp claws. They are often dark in color and give off a putrid smell. The cannon-ball tree has special spikes for bats to hang onto while they feed.

Insects are particularly attracted to blue or yellow flowers and to flowers with a fragrant scent. Bees have short tongues and visit flowers where the nectar is fairly near the surface. Butterflies, on the other hand, have very long tongues and the flowers that they visit have their nectar at the base of very long slender tubes.

Flowers that are pollinated by birds do not produce scent as birds have a poor sense of smell. They are usually brightly colored in a range of reds and oranges.

▼ *Most tropical trees produce* **cauliflorus** *flowers that burst through their trunks. The strength of the trunk allows the trees to produce heavy seeds, like these cocoa pods and breadfruit, which contain plenty of nutrients for the young seedlings.*

cocoa

breadfruit

HUMMINGBIRDS

*B**irds too are heavy to land on flowers and hummingbirds have perfected the art of hovering in front of the flowers as they feed. They sip the nectar with their long beaks and tongues that can reach deep into the flowers. In order to hover, they have to beat their wings as much as 100 times a second! Their ability to hover means that they can feed from flowers that would be too delicate to bear their weight.*

Seed Dispersal

Once a plant has been pollinated, seeds will form which contain everything that is necessary to produce a new plant. Besides the embryo plant, the seed often contains a food store which will help the germinating seedling to grow.

◄ *Fruit bats press fruit against a horny ridge in their mouths to extract the juice.*

▼ *Toucans and parrots have strong beaks to tear the flesh of fruit and to crack nuts.*

For the seedling to get the best chance in life it is important that it does not grow too close to the parent plant and have to compete with it for sunlight, water and nutrients. There has to be some way to ensure that the seeds are scattered over as wide an area as possible, and plants have developed many different ways of doing this.

Wind and water

Emergent trees raise their branches above the canopy, and here there is enough wind to carry the seeds away across the tree tops. The seeds of the emergent trees may be covered in fluff or have projecting wings or scales to catch the wind.

The seeds of epiphytes are airborne, so they produce very tiny seeds that are so light that they float about like dust and can be spread by even the slightest air movement. Some orchids, for instance, have the smallest of all seeds, and it may take as many as 3,000,000 of them to weigh 0.03 oz (1 gram)!

Plants that grow near water often use it to disperse their seeds. The seeds need to be able to float and to be tough enough to withstand the water flow. Seeds of water-lilies, for example, have air pockets inside them so that they can float away from the parent plants. When the seeds become waterlogged, they sink to the bottom of the stream, where they germinate and grow into new plants.

Explosive seed pods

Some plants have seed pods that break open with explosive force, scattering the seeds for some distance. The monkey's dinnerbell *Hura crepitans* is such a plant. It gets its name from the noise made as the pods split open. The seeds can be thrown up to 50 feet (15 meters).

Fruits for animals

Most tropical plants rely on animals to disperse their seeds. They do this by wrapping the seeds inside fruits which are eaten by fruit-eating creatures. Fruits remain inconspicuous until the seeds are ripe, then they become brightly colored or scented to advertise the fact that they are ready to be eaten. The seeds may be scattered as the animal feeds, or they may pass through the digestive system and pass out with the animal's droppings.

PARTICULAR PARASITE PROBLEMS

*P*arasitic plants have a special problem. *It is not enough that their seeds are scattered, they need to be attached to a suitable host plant or they cannot grow. Mistletoe seeds, for instance, are sticky and contain a strong laxative substance. Mistletoe birds eat the seeds and quickly pass them out with their droppings. The seeds stick to the birds, who get rid of them by rubbing against a branch. This deposits the seeds in an ideal place for it to grow.*

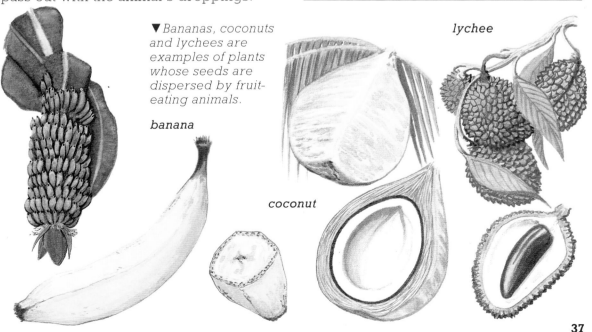

▼ *Bananas, coconuts and lychees are examples of plants whose seeds are dispersed by fruit-eating animals.*

banana

lychee

coconut

Cloud and Seasonal Forests

Mountain ranges occur in tropical areas, as they do everywhere else in the world. In the lowland areas, hot and steamy rain forests grow, but the temperature cools and the vegetation changes as you climb higher up into the mountains.

As the air becomes cooler, there is more rainfall, but the plants do not benefit from this extra water. The soil becomes more sandy or gravelly. Water drains away quickly and the soil becomes dry in spite of the heavy rainfall. Here the soil will not be rich in nutrients because most of them are washed down to the lowland areas. The vegetation becomes less abundant the higher you go.

Water conservation

Trees tend to be smaller and to grow less well and, as the soil is dry, plants have to conserve water. Many of them have small, leathery leaves to reduce transpiration (see p. 11). The trees are usually draped with mosses, liverworts and other epiphytes, and these often send roots down into the soil so that they can get more water and nutrients. Bromeliads grow well in this harsh environment for their rosette cups hold a reserve of water.

Seasonal or monsoon forests

As you move away from the equator, the climate becomes more seasonal. Instead of it being hot and wet all of the time, there are drier periods that alternate with intense monsoon rains.

Monsoon forest trees are shorter and more widely spaced than rain forest trees. They are also more deeply rooted and often have much thicker protective bark. More and more deciduous trees grow farther away from the equator. Seasonal forest trees lose their leaves, however, because of the hot dry periods and not, as in temperate woodland, because of cold winters. The sparser, more widely

▼ *When the seasonal forest trees lose their leaves, plants on the ground enjoy the extra light. Many of them rely on this period to make their main spurt of growth.*

▶ *Conifers, such as Podocarpus, abound in cloud forests. Their narrow, rolled leaves help to reduce water loss.*

MORE LIGHT FOR GROUND PLANTS

*B*ecause the trees are small and sparse, more light reaches the ground here than in the rain forests lower down. Ferns, mosses, bromeliads and climbing plants ramble over the rocks, forming a dense green carpet. Plants that are normally small herbs can sometimes reach enormous proportions - such as daisies that grow 16 feet (5 meters) tall!

spaced trees allow more light to reach the forest floor, where a continuous lush covering of plants grow.

Another kind of vegetation is found on some tropical islands, such as Hawaii and the Galapagos. These are islands that have been formed by volcanic activity and their plants have developed quite separately from the plants on the mainland. They are often unique, being found nowhere else but on their particular island.

▶*Some island plants are unique to their island. In Hawaii, Ohia trees grow in the Alakai swamps, where there is over 400 inches (1,016 cm) of rain a year. They are hard to see except when bearing their scarlet blooms, for they are completely covered with epiphytes. In the Galapagos Islands stunted trees,* Scalesia incisa *and* Scalesia affinis *gain a foothold on the volcanic rock.*

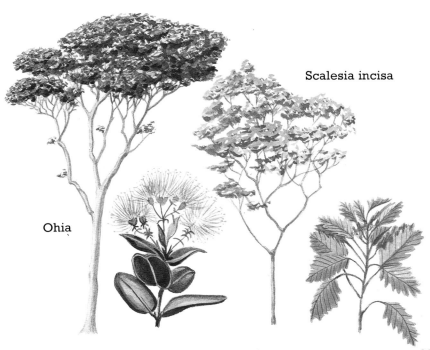

Scalesia incisa

Ohia

Bamboo Forests and Riverbanks

Bamboos are very large grasses and are found in tropical and subtropical regions of Asia, Africa and Australia. They are primitive grasses and grow in large, dense groves.

There are many species of bamboo, some of them are very tall. The tallest of all is *Dendrocalamus giganteus* from Malaysia, which has stems 120 feet (36.5 meters) tall.

Bamboo leaves are long and narrow and their stems are straight and hollow. The stems are divided into sections by swollen joints, called **nodes**. The stem tissue contains silica, which makes them very strong and shiny.

Bamboo stems are used for all sorts of purposes. Large ones are used in house building, piping and furniture, and musical instruments can be made out of them. Thin ones are woven into baskets.

The ways bamboo grows

There are two main groups of bamboo which differ in the way they grow. Both groups produce new plants from small buds formed on swollen underground

▲ *Bamboos can form such dense growth that it is almost impossible for any other plants to grow among them.*

▼ *Bamboos usually reproduce by budding from underground rhizomes.*

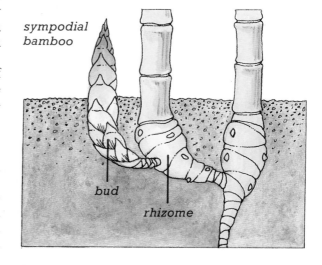

sympodial bamboo

bud

rhizome

stems or **rhizomes**. As with all grasses, these rhizomes allow the plants to spread and colonize an area, preventing other plants from growing close by.

In monopodial bamboos the rhizomes are long and thin. The buds are widely spaced and the new plants are well spread out. Sympodial bamboos have short rhizomes, the buds are close together and the new plants that grow from them are arranged in clumps.

Bamboos have the fastest growth rate of any plant - one species in Kew Gardens in England was recorded as growing 3 feet (1 meter) in 24 hours! Such rapid growth causes bamboos to make loud and eerie noises as they grow upward. Many a traveler has been frightened by these weird, ghostly sounds coming from the bamboo forests.

Rare flowers

Bamboos reproduce **vegetatively** by growing new plants from their rhizomes. They rarely reproduce sexually, by producing flowers. Some species only bloom once every 60 or 100 years and then every member of the same species flowers at the same time. This process uses up so much energy that the mature plants die as soon as the seeds have ripened. All that is left are seeds and seedlings to re-establish the bamboo forest.

This can be a disaster for animals that rely on bamboo as their main source of food. For example, the giant panda is an animal that only eats bamboo. The panda was recently threatened with extinction in one particular area of China when all the bamboo plants there flowered and died, leaving the pandas with nothing to eat.

The edge of riverbanks

Just as bamboos can form an almost impenetrable screen of vegetation, so can the plants that grow alongside the edge of a riverbank. A river causes a break in the continuous forest canopy and allows the light to flood in. Plants that are normally low-growing or stunted in the gloom of the forest floor thrive in the light, warmth and wetness of the riverbank. They sometimes grow to enormous proportions.

▶ *Riverbank growth is the thickest to be seen anywhere in the world. The narrow leaves of palms and the divided leaves of the Swiss cheese plant are not damaged by rapidly flowing water. Epiphytes grow long aerial roots that dangle in the river below and the banks are bright with the red and yellow fruits of climbing cucumbers.*

Mangrove Swamps

In some places, tropical forests grow right down to the sea. The trees that grow in these saltwater swamps are called mangroves. These swamps are a rich source of unique animal and plant life.

Strictly speaking, the word mangrove applies only to the 60 or so species of *Rhizophora*, but it is often used to describe any of the trees that grow in tidal swamps.

From sea to dry land

Mangroves are "coastline builders." All sorts of debris collects around their roots and gradually builds up into a layer of rich mud that rises above water level. The red mangrove, for instance, takes root in the water, but is left high and dry when the mud rises around its roots. Eventually it dies out and its place is taken by black or white mangroves that are less dependent on water for their living. In this way, the swamps are slowly transformed into dry land, and the coastline is pushed gradually farther out to sea.

Problems with salt

Mangrove trees are rooted in salt water, so they are constantly absorbing salt, which is carried up to their leaves. Too

◄*Mangroves develop aerial roots that slant down in a tangled mass from their trunks to help anchor and support them in the moving water. As the old roots become silted over by the rising layer of mud, new roots grow from higher up in the tree.*

►*Swamp cypresses have pneumatophores, described as "knobbly knees," that may rise 10 feet (3 meters) up in the air. When these structures die with age, they become hollow. Black mangroves grow finger-like projections, about $\frac{1}{2}$ inch (1 cm) thick, from their submerged roots.*

much salt is poisonous for plants, and some way has to be found to get rid of it. The leaves of mangroves are able to excrete salt onto their surface. The salt is washed away by rain, or it dissolves in the humid atmosphere. Some mangroves store the salt in their leaves. They then shed the old leaves and grow new ones.

Quick-grow seeds

The seeds of mangroves start to grow their roots while they are still attached to the parent plant. When they are ready, the seeds fall into water that is constantly moving with the tides. Sometimes they sink immediately, but they may be carried for some distance by the tide.

As they already have their early roots, the seedlings can anchor themselves quickly, as soon as they become lodged in a suitable place. In this way they avoid being carried hither and thither by the ever-moving water.

Breathing roots

Roots that are submerged in water or in waterlogged mud soon become deprived of oxygen, and "drown." Plant roots normally grow downwards into the soil, but mangroves have extra, special roots that defy gravity and instead grow upwards out of the water into the air. These are breathing roots, called **pneumatophores**. They have large "breathing" pores called **lenticils** through which they absorb oxygen. The oxygen then passes through a fine network of air passages, to the roots in the water.

THE LARGEST LEAVES IN THE WORLD

The giant water-lily, Victoria regia, grows in still backwaters of the Amazon forest. It has the largest leaves in the world. They are circular, can weigh over 198 lbs (90 kg) and can reach 7 feet (2 meters) across. The edges of the leaves turn up, forming a rim. Underneath there is an amazing network of raised ribs which gives the leaf great strength and supports large air pockets that enable the leaves to float. The plant has large pale flowers which gives off a powerful scent at night. They are pollinated by beetles.

Tropical Partnerships

Tropical forests are heavily populated, complex places where plants and animals are often dependent on one another and form partnerships.

Orchids, for instance, have very tiny seeds which do not contain enough food for the seedlings to start life on their own. Orchid seedlings can only grow properly when they are in partnership with a fungus, usually *Rhizoctonia*. The fungus provides the orchid seedling with food and vitamins so that it can get established. The fungus then grows into the orchid's roots. The fungus and the orchid exchange nutrients, giving and taking from each other the essential foods that they cannot obtain for themselves.

The "fixing" of nitrogen

For another example of a partnership, we must go to the cloud forests. Most cloud forest plants have small leaves, but there

▲ *A hungry* Hymenopus *mantis looks like an innocent flower as it waits to grab an unsuspecting beefly.*

▶ *Thorn bugs suck the sap from their host plants and grow to look like thorns.*

▶ *Female fig wasps fertilize the hidden female flowers as they lay their eggs on the ovaries of the flower.*

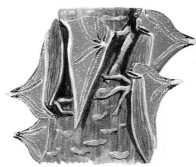

is one outstanding exception. This is a plant called *Gunnera* which has enormous leaves. It has formed a partnership with a blue-green alga which lives in the plant tissue at the base of its leaves.

Normally plants can only get their nitrogen from the soil in the form of nitrates. However, some of the very minute, single-celled organisms like these algae and some bacteria, can "fix" nitrogen from the air. This means that they can combine nitrogen gas with other substances to form the nitrates that plants need for their food. The *Gunnera* therefore keeps its own "fertilizer factory" in its leaves and is able to grow well in poor soil.

Figs and their wasps

There are over 900 species of figs, ranging from small epiphytes to climbers and large trees. All of them have an association with small wasps and each species of fig has its own particular species of wasp.

The fig flower never appears on the outside of the plant, but remains within the fruit or fig. When the flower is ready to be pollinated, it releases a scent which attracts the female wasp to a small opening at the base of the fruit. The tiny female wasp crawls through this hole, losing her

PLANT LOOK-ALIKES

Some plants grow to look like insects so that they attract other insects to pollinate them (see p. 34). This mimicry can work the other way round and some animals grow to look like plants. Green tree frogs, leaf insects and stick insects are some of the creatures that use this sort of camouflage to hide from their enemies.

wings and antennae as she goes. Once inside, she lays her eggs on the ovaries of the female flowers. At the same time she transfers pollen brought with her to the stigma so that the seeds start to grow.

The wasp grubs feed on the seeds and eventually turn into male and female wasps that mate with each other. The males leave the fruit first by boring their way out. As they do this, air is allowed inside the fruit and the male flowers now open. The female wasps then make their escape, becoming covered with pollen as they do so. Once the last of the wasps has left, the fruit ripens, ready to be eaten and the remaining seeds are scattered. The little female wasps, covered in pollen, fly to another fig flower, crawl inside and start the whole circle of life over again.

Plants and Ants

Plants are eaten by many sorts of animals, from small insect grubs and caterpillars to large grazing herbivores. Many have developed ways of fending off these grazers and preventing themselves from being eaten. Some even use ants as "guardians" to protect them.

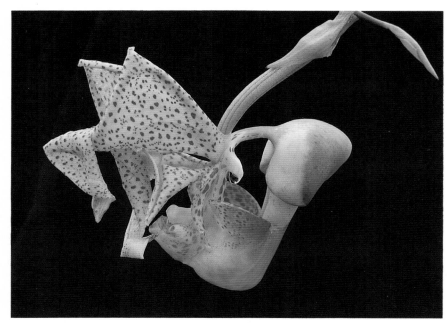

◄ *Bucket orchids are almost impossible to cultivate if ants are not present.*

▶ *Some ants are "farmers" and keep scale insects for the sake of the sweet honeydew that they exude. Some branches provide a home not only for ants but also for their scale insects.*

In tropical areas ants are abundant and they can be found almost everywhere. Throughout history, plants and ants have not only lived together but have formed a relationship from which both partners benefit. This type of association is called **mutualism**. It is so common, particularly in the tropics, that certain "ant plants" have been given the name **myrmecophytes**.

Ants as bodyguards

One way that plants protect themselves from being eaten is to produce poisonous substances to make themselves so distasteful that animals leave them alone. Another way is to employ insects such as ants to defend them.

The plants provide food and shelter for the ants, which then establish their colony in or around the plants and defend it as their territory. Ant colonies may be built in any part of the plant – in bulbs, corms or rhizomes, leaves, roots, stems, palm fronds, within pitchers or even within large thorns.

Fearsome warning

Ants can be very fierce in defense of their territory and even large animals are justly frightened of them. Some colonies have special guard ants which raise the alarm by beating their jaws together. This alarm call is taken up by other ants and soon the whole colony is on the alert. The sound of the alarm is usually enough to frighten off the intruder, but if not the ants will mount a vicious attack, biting and stinging the unfortunate animal.

Ant acacias

Ant acacias are found throughout the tropics. They do not have any means of defense against grazing animals and rely solely on ants to do this job. The ants are attracted to sweet nectar that is produced in special glands, called nectaries, at the base of the leaf stalks. The plants also have swellings at the tips of their leaves. These contain proteins and vitamins that are essential for the growth of the young ants.

The ants establish their colonies so that they are close to this food supply. They hollow out the long thorns of the tree and live inside them. Any animal that comes too close to the plant will be attacked. Even large monkeys tend to avoid the trees that have ant guardians.

The ants do an extra service for the trees. They prune back any vine or branch that grows too close and remove any seeds from around the trunk. In this way the ants keep a space clear around their tree and prevent other plants from shading or competing with it.

A PITCHER FULL OF ANTS

*D*ischidia *is a tiny pitcher plant. Instead of trapping insects inside its pitchers it uses them as containers for ant colonies. The plant is protected by the ants, but it gets an additional benefit. It grows little rootlets from its leaf stalks that penetrate into its own pitchers and take nutrients from the debris left behind by the ants.*

▼Myrmecodia *is an epiphyte from Southeast Asia. It grows tubers that can be 1 foot (30 cm) long and 8 inches (20 cm) across. These are riddled with ant galleries. Some of the tunnels are used by the ants to store waste debris and this provides valuable minerals which the plant absorbs.*

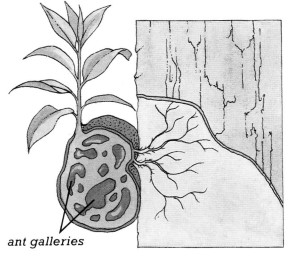

ant galleries

Plants That Eat Animals

Ⓞne of the substances that is essential for plants is nitrogen, and they absorb it in the form of nitrogenous compounds from the soil, through their roots.

◀ *The pitcher plant,* Nepenthes, *attracts insects to its brightly colored trap.*

In some situations it is difficult for plants to get enough nitrogen. It may be because they are epiphytes and water and nutrients are always in short supply. It may be that they grow in bogs or swamps where the acid, waterlogged or peaty soil is deficient in nitrogen, making it hard for plants to grow there. It is made worse if they are competing against thick growths of sphagnum moss, which quickly sucks up most of the available nutrients.

Finding enough nitrogen

Plants that have to contend with this problem often make use of an alternative source of nitrogen – the bodies of insects and other small creatures. These plants are carnivorous, that is they feed on the bodies of animals. If they feed on insects, they are called insectivorous.

The success of these plants depends on their ability to attract and capture their prey and they have developed some quite remarkable lures and traps. The plants produce a liquid that contains acids and enzymes which kills and digests the animals' bodies. This provides the much needed nitrogen which the plant absorbs and uses for its growth.

Pitfall traps

The simplest type of trap is the pitfall trap of the sort used by the pitcher plant. Their leaves are modified to form deep pitchers in which insects and small animals drown. These plants lure their victims with sweet-smelling nectar and brightly colored pitchers. The doomed creatures hope for a tasty meal but instead they find themselves on a slippery slope down which they slide into the enzyme "soup" below.

Darlingtonia californica is called the cobra lily because it looks very like a cobra, reared up and ready to strike. What looks like a forked "tongue" provides a landing place for insects, which are attracted into the "eyes" by the scent of the nectar. Once inside, the insects fall into the pitcher below. The trapped insects try to escape through "windows" in the top of the pitcher, but they only fall back again into the trap.

Flypaper traps

The leaves of butterworts have special glands that produce a sticky fluid. Once an insect is caught, the leaf slowly folds round it so that it cannot escape. The plants then produce enzymes to digest the trapped insect.

Suction traps

Bladderworts have leaves that are modified into hollow bladders. These bladders have trapdoors that open when an animal brushes past. The prey is sucked into the bladder and is trapped when the door closes behind it. Some bladderworts grow in the ponds of bromeliads, feeding on the small creatures living there.

▼ *Pinguicula caerula is a butterwort that grows in the Florida Everglades and traps insects on its sticky leaves.*

The floating waterwheel plant, Aldrovanda, is found in Europe as well as in tropical Africa. Its jointed leaves are covered in tiny, sensitive hairs that are stimulated if an insect lands on them. The leaves then snap shut – like a giant clam!

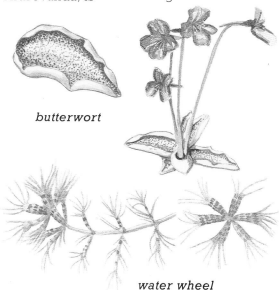

butterwort

water wheel

▼ *Some fungi also obtain their food from animals. A rotifer biting one of these fungi will be stuck fast and suffocated.*

An eelworm that ventures into a fungus noose will be strangled when the noose suddenly tightens.

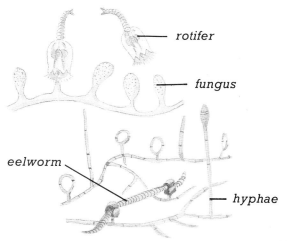

rotifer

fungus

eelworm

hyphae

Tropical Houseplants

Plants have perhaps always been appreciated for their beauty, but it was the Chinese who first cultivated them for decorative use as long ago as 2000 BC.

During the sixteenth and seventeenth centuries, western people also began to grow plants for pleasure, and this trend soon caught on. Today, barely a home, bank, hotel or other public place is without some sort of plant display.

Many of these plants have their origins in the tropics and, although some require very careful handling to re-create their original habitat, many can survive in modern homes. Their restful appearance and sometimes exotic scent are often much appreciated.

Make your plants at home

A plant in a pot does not grow naturally and you will only get healthy plants by trying, as near as possible, to reproduce its natural environment. Plants must be

▲ *The goosefoot plant,* Syngonium, *is a climber which can be displayed growing up a moss pole.*

◀ *The passion flower,* Passiflora caerulea, *produces splendid blooms and is best grown around a wire hoop.*

checked regularly to make sure that their roots have enough room and they should be moved to a bigger pot if necessary. While the plant is growing rapidly, there are special plant foods that should be added to the soil in the pot. They should also be checked for pests and diseases and you can ask in your local store for a suitable insecticide.

Imitate the dimness and dampness of the forest

Most tropical plants grow beneath the forest canopy, where they are used to shade, warmth and humidity. Think of the conditions in the forest and try to make a "mini environment" as much like that as possible. Protect the plant from strong sunlight and make the air around it humid by surrounding the pot with dampened moss. Spraying the plant with water every day will prevent the leaves from drying out and will also keep the stomata free from household dust.

Fun plants from the kitchen

There are many beautiful tropical plants that can be grown from kitchen scraps. The tops of pineapples can be removed, dried overnight and rooted in moist peat. Seeds from fresh figs germinate easily in a warm place. Date pits, put in a pot covered with plastic and placed in an airing cupboard, will grow into splendid palm plants.

Unroasted coffee beans will produce a shiny-leaved coffee bush. An avocado pit suspended over a thin layer of water will eventually grow roots and can then be planted in a pot.

▶ *The creeping fig,* Ficus pumila, *trails from a hanging pot.* Columnea *or goldfish plant is an epiphyte that trails and produces orange "goldfish" flowers.*

A FOREST IN A BOTTLE

*S*ome tropical plants that are difficult to grow in ordinary pots are particularly suited to "bottle gardens." Any large jar with a lid can be made into a bottle garden. At the bottom of the jar put a layer of gravel, to provide drainage for the roots. Then a layer of charcoal, which will help to keep the bottle fresh. On top of this put some peat-based compost for the roots to grow in. As the bottle garden is enclosed, it is always humid. Keep it in a shady, warm place and it will be like a little bit of the forest floor!

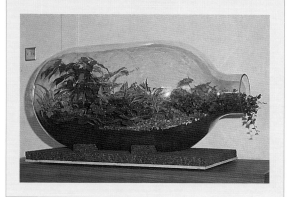

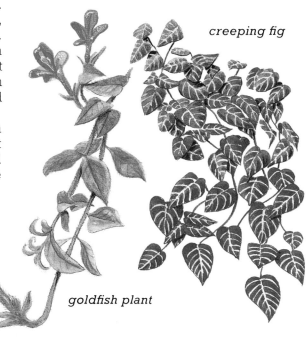

creeping fig

goldfish plant

People of the Forests

Forest tribes have lived almost undisturbed for centuries. They have learned, from knowledge handed down through the generations, to understand and respect the tropical forest that is their home. They depend on the forest, which provides for almost all of their needs.

These people find all their food in the forest. They hunt the wild animals and gather fruit, nuts, roots and leaves. Not only does it give them food, the forest also provides them with fibers for making clothes and baskets, timber for building their homes and drugs and medicines for curing their illnesses. The many rivers provide drinking water, and a means of transport from one part of the forest to another.

Small-scale farming

Farming, where it occurs, tends to be a very temporary affair. The soil of the forest is not very rich in nutrients and can usually only support two or three crops before it becomes completely infertile.

Many of the natives are farmers, but they rely on a technique called "slash and burn." Small areas of forest are cleared and the trees and bushes burned. The ash from the fires releases some nutrients and it is possible to grow crops for two or three years. After that, the people have to gather together their few possessions and move on to another area. The old clearing is left to regenerate its forest cover, but this is a slow process, taking many years.

The forest has a very high humidity, so it is impossible to store food. The crops that are grown in these clearings are mostly root crops that can be left in the ground

▶ *The original tappers who collected latex from wild rubber trees in the forest could not cope with the modern demand for rubber.*

◀ *The forest gives way to grazing cattle to satisfy the world's meat markets. The top soil gets washed away and the land is overgrazed, leading to new deserts.*

until they are needed. Manioc, from which cassava and tapioca are made, yams, sweet potatoes and maize are all important food crops for these farmers.

The arrival of the settled farmers

All over the world, forest boundaries are gradually being pushed back to make room for settled farmers. In much of Asia, this has been going on for centuries but modern methods of transport have opened up even the interior of forests to

mechanical diggers and felling machinery. The process of forest destruction has speeded up alarmingly.

At first, areas were cleared to grow crops like cocoa, oil and fruit. Then rubber became important to modern technology and the wild rubber trees were too few to satisfy the demand. Rubber trees began to be cultivated and now huge areas are given over to rubber plantations. More forest has been cut down and destroyed to make way for huge cattle ranches.

THE DYING TRIBES OF THE FOREST

*A*s the forests are becoming eroded and invaded by roads and townships, the original inhabitants become more and more vulnerable. They are forced to live in increasingly smaller areas which are not always sufficient for their needs. They become victims of diseases brought in by settlers, to which they have no natural resistance. They imitate the new lifestyles and forget their old ways. The destruction of their forest home and the loss of their lifestyles has brought disaster to many of the forest tribes. Sometimes whole tribes have died out.

The Forest Harvest

Plants from the forest have been used for hundreds of years and valuable products are made out of them. However, as world demand increases, larger areas are being cultivated.

For the forest native, these products have grown on his doorstep and have been used by him from time immemorial. Other people have had to discover these plants and learn their value by experiment and exploration.

Many plants are still harvested from their wild environment. However, as demand for these products increases, more and more are being cultivated and grown on plantations, in areas cleared of forest vegetation.

Uses for timber

The timber resources of the rain forests are enormous and include trees of great value, like mahogany and teak, whose wood is highly prized for its beauty and strength. Within the forest, these trees seldom grow close together and harvesting them has been an expensive business – until now. Modern methods of transport, using helicopters to locate valuable trees and trucks to transport them, has made the harvesting of this timber more economic. Many hardwoods from the forests are used in the building industry, while less valuable timber is made into plywood or pulped for paper.

Another way in which we use wood is in the form of charcoal. Charcoal is made by partly burning wood in the absence of air, so that pure carbon is produced.

◄ *The seeds of the cocoa tree are enclosed in a pod. The whole pod is fermented for six days before the seeds are extracted and dried in the sun. At the factory, the seeds are roasted and ground to make cocoa and chocolate.*

The best known use for charcoal is as a domestic fuel, in ovens, barbecues and grills. It has, however, many important industrial uses – in purifying many metals, in fish factories, in cement manufacture and for filtering and purifying water.

The sap that makes rubber

Rubber is still very important to modern industry. In the wild, rubber trees originated in Brazil, but they are now cultivated in plantations in Indonesia, Malaya, Sri Lanka, Thailand and West Africa. Rubber is made from the sap, or latex, which is tapped from the tree through diagonal grooves cut in the bark, allowing the latex to drip into cups.

Plantations of forest trees

People's interest in the fruits of the forest has led them to grow many other valuable trees in plantations, often far away from their original home.

Theobroma cacao, the cocoa tree, originated in South America where the native Indians have always prized its seeds. In the sixteenth century the Spanish introduced cocoa to the rest of the world. It is now grown in plantations in many tropical countries, with Ghana as the world's largest producer today.

Coffee, from the shrub *Coffea arabica*, originated in Africa. It is another example of a widely cultivated plant, prized for its seeds. Today, Brazil is the world's largest producer of coffee, although much still comes from Africa.

The oil palm, *Elaeis guineensis*, also originated in Africa, but there are now plantations in Malaysia and Indonesia. This tall palm has bright red fruit the oil of which is used to make margarine and soap.

Another plantation crop is sugarcane, a tall bamboo-like grass that originated in Southeast Asia. It has been cultivated from ancient times and now grows in plantations in South America, the West Indies and Australia.

TROPICAL TREASURE TROVE

The tropics gives us many valuable products for our homes and industry – These include many exotic fruits and vegetables found in supermarkets as well as fibers, spices and medicines. How many more can you discover?

Fruits and vegetables 	papayas; lychees; mangoes; passion fruit; yam; bread fruit; bananas
Fibers	cotton; kapok; jute
Gums and oils	gum arabic; patchouli
Spices	allspice; nutmeg; cloves; vanilla
Pharma-ceuticals	quinine; strychnine

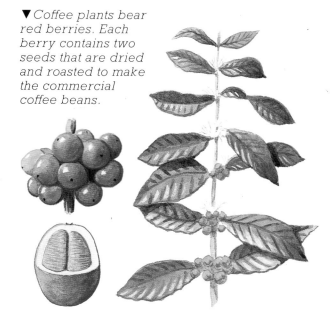

▼ *Coffee plants bear red berries. Each berry contains two seeds that are dried and roasted to make the commercial coffee beans.*

55

Destruction of the Forests

The forests are being destroyed at an alarming rate. In recent years, over 6200 miles (10,000 km) of roads have been driven into the Amazon forest alone. Each year an area the size of Florida is being stripped of trees.

◀ *The forests of the world remove the carbon dioxide that we release into the air, from our fires and generators, our factory chimneys, our automobiles and our breathing.*

▶ *Our forests and the plants in them are precious to us all. Without them the very existence of our world is threatened.*

Although many people are aware that this destruction is taking place, they do not always realize just how serious the result might be. They are also unaware how difficult it is to put a stop to it.

Poverty leads to destruction

Many of the countries in the tropics are poor and the people are only making use of their most valuable asset, the forest itself, to bring them what we all want – a decent standard of living. In the past, people did the same with the vast forests of Europe and North America – used them for their own ends, and destroyed them. It is hard to blame the people in undeveloped countries for doing the same thing. However, the consequences of this destruction are so grave and far-reaching that somehow it must be prevented.

Forests turn to deserts

It is not enough to fell fewer trees and hope that the forest regenerates itself to its former state. As we have already seen, the soil of the forest is poor and most of the nutrients are in the timber itself. Remove the timber and you remove the nutrients. Let the plant roots die and there is nothing to hold the soil together and prevent it from being completely washed away. Once the forest growth is lost, the area becomes almost completely infertile and unable to recover.

The effect on climate

The millions of forest trees are the great rain makers of the world. Constantly drawing water from their roots, they release it through their leaves. The hot air,

heavy with moisture, rises as great rain clouds, to send torrential rains back on to the forest below.

Without the trees the land is without rain and eventually desert conditions replace the once lush forest. Many of the droughts and famines seen in Africa today are thought to be due to the destruction of the trees in the savanna.

The lost resources

When the forest homes are destroyed the people's tribal way of life is spoiled. Much of the old knowledge is lost, and the plants and animals that are their food and medicines die out.

It has been estimated that only one-sixth of the species of the tropics have been named. Many of them yield valuable plant strains that enrich our agriculture, and drugs that form the basis of our medicines. Who knows how many precious foods and drugs have yet to be discovered – and perhaps lost before they are ever known?

The effect on us all

The forests are often called the "lungs of the world." The oxygen that people breathe comes to us from the plant world, through the process of photosynthesis. The tropical forests give the world the oxygen that we need – and they also remove the carbon dioxide from the air. Too much carbon dioxide could cause one of the greatest hazards to modern man – the "greenhouse effect." The raising of the air temperatures, the melting of the polar ice caps, the raising of the sea levels and a change of climate could spell disaster for the world.

57

Glossary

Annual A plant that completes its entire life cycle within one year; from germination of a seed to the production of more seeds.

Bulb A swollen underground structure that is an organ of both food storage and vegetative reproduction. Bulbs consist of a modified shoot with a shortened stem which is enclosed by fleshy scalelike leaves.

Cauliflorus Flowers that are borne on thick stems or trunks of trees. These types of flowers are produced almost exclusively by trees of the tropical rainforests.

Chlorophyll A green pigment found in algae and higher plants. It is used to trap the sun's energy which is required to make sugar from carbon dioxide gas and water during photosynthesis.

Epiphyte A plant that grows on another plant, but which does not take anything from it other than support.

Evaporate A process by which water is turned into gas and water vapor and lost into the air.

Fertilization The fusion of a male cell with a female cell to form a seed.

Haustoria A rootlike structure that penetrates the cells of a host plant, taking food and water from it.

Hyphae (singular hypha) The threads or strands that form the body of a fungus.

Lenticel A small breathing hole in the woody tissue of a plant through which the exchange of gases can take place.

Microphyll A small simple leaf produced by such plants as clubmosses, horsetails and lichens.

Monocarpic A plant that flowers just once during its entire lifetime.

Mutualism An association between two living organisms which is beneficial to both partners.

Mycelium The main "feeding body" of a fungus which is made up of many hyphae.

Myrmecophytes Plants that form a relationship with ants from which both plant and ant benefit.

Nodes The part of the stem from which buds or leaves arise. The portion of stem between the nodes is called the internode.

Ovule The female part of a flower that develops into a seed after fertilization has taken place.

Parasite A plant or animal that is unable to provide its own food and so gets all its food from another animal or plant – its host.

Phloem Specialized cells that transport food made in the leaves around a plant.

Photosynthesis The process by which green plants convert carbon dioxide gas and water into sugar and oxygen. The energy required for the reaction is obtained from sunlight.

Pneumatophore A specialized breathing root which, unlike most roots, grows upwards. It is produced by plants that inhabit swampy areas.

Pollen Tiny grains produced by higher plants which contain the male sex cells.

Pollination The act of transferring the male cells or pollen from the stamen to the female stigma.

Pulvinus An enlarged area at the base of a leaf stalk which can rotate the leaf in response to light.

Rhizome An organ that stores food and can also produce new plants by vegetative reproduction. Food reserves are built up in a swollen underground stem. New plants grow from buds which arise where the reduced scalelike leaves join the stem.

Saprophyte An organism that feeds on dead and decaying plants or animals.

Seed The fully developed, fertilized ovule. It contains an embryo and often a store of food, and can germinate and grow into a new plant.

Sexual reproduction The fusing of a male cell with a female cell to produce a new individual.

Stamen The male reproductive organ of a flower. It is made up of a filament and an anther which contains pollen.

Stigma The part of a plant's female reproductive organ, the carpel, on which pollen lands.

Stomata (singular stoma) A small hole or pore on the surface of a leaf, which allows gases and water vapor to move into and out of the cells during respiration and photosynthesis.

Style The stem that supports the stigma.

Transpiration The loss of water vapor from a plant, through the stomata, due to evaporation.

Trichomes Small flaps on the leaf surface that can open or shut to allow water into and out of cells. They are often found at the base of leaves which form the water holding reservoir of the urn plants or bromeliads and allow the plant to take water from its own water reserves.

Vegetative reproduction Asexual reproduction in which a small part of the parent plant becomes detached and forms a new plant. New plants can also form from underground bulbs, corms, tubers or rhizomes.

Velamen A layer of dead cells which surrounds and protects the tips of aerial roots. These cells can absorb water and conduct it to the live cells beneath.

Xylem Specialized cells which transport water and mineral salts around a plant.

Index

Further Reading

Young Adult Books – Tropical Plants

Burnie, David. *Tree*. New York: Alfred A. Knopf, 1988.

Reidman, Sarah. *Trees Alive*. New York: Lothrop, Lee & Shepard, 1974.

Young Adult Books – General

Black, David. *Plants*. New York: Facts On File, 1986.

Forsthoeful, John. *Discovering Botany* New York: DOK Publishers, 1982.

Lambert, David. *Vegetation*. New York: Franklin Watts, 1984.

Adult Books – Tropical Plants

Jamieson, B.G. *Tropical Plant Types*. Pergamon Press, 1967.

Lotschert, William. *The Collins Guide to Tropical Plants*. New York: Viking Penguin, 1989.

Steenfoft, Margaret. *Tropical Plant Biology*. South Asia Books, 1988

Adult Books – General Reference about Botany

New England Wild Flower Society Staff. *Botany for All Ages*. New Jersey: Globe Pequot Press, 1989.

Rost, Thomas L. Botany: *A Brief Introduction to Plant Biology*. New York: John Willey & Sons, 1984.

Tootill, Elizabeth (ed.). *The Facts On File Dictionary of Botany*. New York: Facts On File, 1984.

Photographic credits

t = top, *b* = bottom, *l* = left, *r* = right

Cover: Frank Lane/Silvestris; page 6 Frank Lane/Silvestris; page 7 Frank Lane/Mark Newman; page 8*l* Frank Lane/Premaphotos Wildlife; page 8*r* Bruce Coleman/Christian Zuber; page 10 G.S.F. Picture Library; page 12*l* Frank Lane/Premaphotos Wildlife; page 12*r* Bruce Coleman/M.P.L. Fogden; page 13 Bruce Coleman/E. and P. Bauer; page 14 Bruce Coleman/F. Erize; page 15 Bruce Coleman/Hans Reinhard; page 16 Frank Lane/Premaphotos Wildlife; page 17 Bruce Coleman/C. and D. Frith; page 18*l* Frank Lane/Rod Martin; page 18*r* Bruce Coleman/ Waina Cheng Ward; page 19 Bruce Coleman/Gerald Cubitt; page 20 Bruce Coleman/L.C. Marigo; page 22 Frank Lane/ G. Moon; page 23 Bruce Coleman/D. and M. Plage; page 24*t* Bruce Coleman/ Hans Reinhard; page 24*b* Bruce Coleman/Norman Tomalin; page 25 Frank Lane/Holt Studios; page 26 Smith/Polunin Collection; page 27 Bruce Coleman/ M.P. Kahl; page 28 Frank Lane/Premaphotos Wildlife; page 29 Frank Lane/Ron Austing; page 30*l* Frank Lane/S.C. Bisserot; page 30*r* Bruce Coleman/D and M. Plage; page 31 Bruce Coleman/P. Ward; page 32 Bruce Coleman/S. Ziesler; page 33 Frank Lane/Mark Newman; page 34 Frank Lane/R. Thompson; page 35 Bruce Coleman/ G.D. Plage; page 36*l* Bruce Coleman/Jane Burton; page 36*r* Frank Lane/Premaphotos Wildlife; page 37 Cyril Laubscher/C. and L. Nature World; page 38 Frank Lane/Holt Studios; page 39*l* Bruce Coleman/Gerald Cubitt; page 39*r* Bruce Coleman/Michael Freeman; page 40 Bruce Coleman/Eric Crichton; page 42 Frank Lane/S.C. Bisserot; page 43 Bruce Coleman/Hans Reinhard; page 44 Frank Lane/Premaphotos Wildlife; page 45 Frank Lane/Premaphotos Wildlife; page 46 John Blowers; page 47*t* Frank Lane/ Premmaphotos Wildlife; page 47*b* Frank Lane/Premaphotos Wildlife; page 48 Frank Lane/Premaphotos Wildlife; page 50*t* Smith/ Polunin collection; page 50*b* Frank Lane/ Silvestris; page 51 Smith/Polunin Collection; page 52 Frank Lane/A.R. Hamblin; page 53*t* Frank Lane/Holt Studios; page 53*b* Frank Lane/S.C. Bisserot; page 54 Bruce Coleman/ M.P.L. Fogden; page 56 Bruce Coleman/ Colin molyneux; page 57 Frank Lane/Holt Studios.